Thank You!

IIIII II IIIII IIIIII III IIII III
I0172911

Post-Publishing Dedication
This book is dedicated to our fellow poet
Mychael Jamoson Greene (Myke G) who
passed away January 2018.

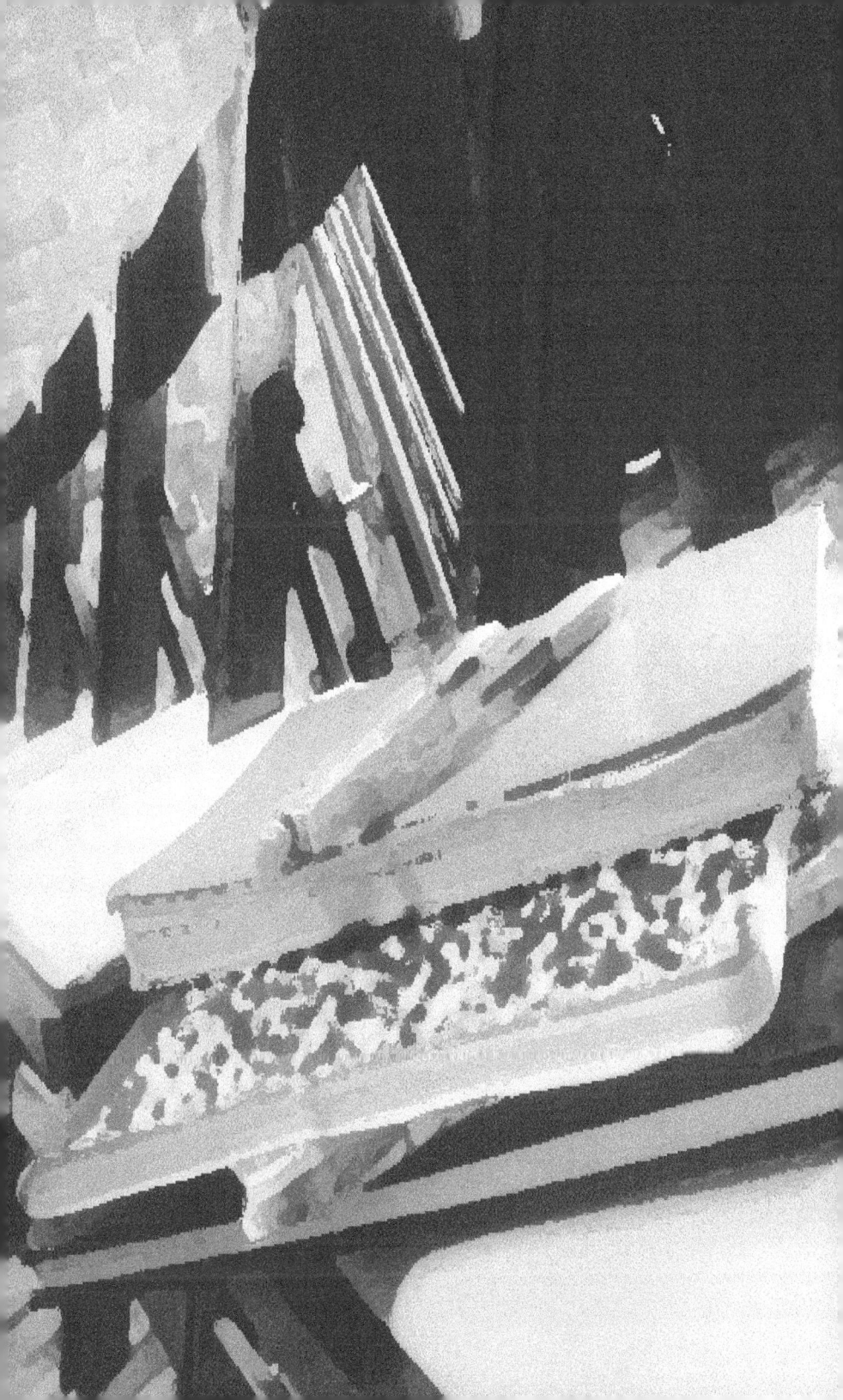

Main St. Mondays

Volume 1

A Collection Poetry & Prose from the Heart of Main Street Chattanooga, TN

Contributing Poets
Erika Blackmon, Mychael Greene,
Marsha Mills, Sarah Platt, Laura Brown,
and Luronda Jennings

Cover Photo: Erika Blackmon

ISBN: 978-1-941749-64-7
4-P Publishing
Chattanooga, TN

Contents

Introduction

Thank you for purchasing our book of poems! Main Street Mondays was developed to help poets, writers and people that want to write, get back to it. Many of the poems in this collection were created, spontaneously, during our meetings during the month of August 2016. The poets will also host a spoken word event highlighting their creations.

For more information about future Main St. Mondays workshops and performances, please contact Erika Blackmon at

dionneblackmon189@gmail.com

Thank you for your support.

Photograph by James Cooley III

Erika Blackmon

Uncharted territory
The heart of the hurt
A dark void
Silenced sentiments
Invisible and internal moans
Captured in an instance
Not recognized by many
Regression has no pleasure
Especially when being regurgitated
Onto silver plates of denial
Total Understanding is required.
~E

*Search honestly against my emotions *
(shame)
I tasted his sorrowful potion...
Made of mirrored stares
Liquid blame
No glass to fill
Just an unwanted glare
Soul having a metaphorical existence
(shame)
Comparing mE to an abstract theory
Trying to embrace or embarrass
Unsure of the game but I know
that it's an awful shame... and
Life will never be the same...
~E

*Note from Erika, the use of "mE" is intentional. It's
symbolic of the uniqueness embodied by mE.*

Homeless words.
No mail to receive
but messages are expected.
Not but a deserted dollar away
from being Poor.
BUT....
A purposeful paintbrush stroke away
from being Rich.
On a pictured canvas
a creative itch.
A priceless painting
producing pennies for the
silent masses
~E

High in the air as aspirations
of the talented can soar...
Poetic breezes magnify the moment
A collaboration meant to happen
A meeting of creatives
Lean bodies
Lean meanings
A gathering
We are here
A gathering
We are here
Let's create...
~E

I am just a piece of paper
Blank but full
of possible potential
to be molded into
Something
remarkable
Something
real
Something
profound
Something courageously created
and given to the eyes of those that need it
in an intense indigo ink...
engraved into the edges of existence
Forgiving fabric of reality
I am just several pieces of precious paper now...
We are greatness...multiplied...~E

A Galaxy Purple -Photograph by James Cooley III

Mychael Greene

C's the Moment

cease the moments
to call yourself a blessing,
careful with the words to not create a
cancer to your spirit but to carry change
to your mother earth, chasing a cheap
thrill will not give you class but
choosing, cleaning, a comfortable
company among those who cling to you
will only bring you a concrete,
courageous, cordial, convenient,
commander which will capitalize you to
be that
Confident, Charismatic, Conqueror
Known as his Queen.

MykeG

Rose Water

(Drop Your Red Roses)

Bloodshed over young heads some young, some old, a flood raises the negative stories of stories never been told, falling in, paralyzed from the waist down I knew I was struggling to live but to wake up and realize I was already standing on my feet, and it was just my thought process that was drowning me, in an ocean with boulders tied to my ankles, surrounded by roses thrown by media predictions, lungs filled with societies beverages with no one around to hear me scream. To realize this rose water isn't made for me to drink but it's made for me to think, to take every damaging comment to show the world that you are not their prisoner but to show them your mind, body, and soul is free.

MykeG

Every Lion Has Its Roar

Hey, beautiful, hey handsome, you're looking good just like God promised. I've prayed for the moment to hold you, love you, and mold you. For the day you can look at the definition of your hands, and I caress your hands and put them on the things you deserve on this earth.

But I got to confess you broke my heart when you cheated on me with doubt and fear that all I could do was cry. I use to listen to your favorite song and watch your horrific dance moves just so you could experience the kiss of happiness, funny thing is I knew this day would come, you need me, crave me, and want me. I'm no one to you, but you're everything to me, who am I?

I'm your goals, confidence, passion but most of all I'm your dreams. So always think of me when you sleep because when you arise just know we both have a testimony and a voice that's used to speak.

MykeG

Stained Glass Emotions

I'm scared of you, ok you win! You could throw a rock at me, but I only know how to stand strong. You constantly kept putting your images of how I walk my daily walk to fit yours, but I still stand strong.

You throw a different tint over me so people can't see the real me because you wanted a "better life for me," thinking my world can't still rhyme with your grades of A's, B's or C's. But for the first time I'm begging you to polish, clean, and wipe away your images of how my life is supposed to be and breathe. Family, Friends, Society, and Media I'm just an imperfect artist made by God that has a message to spread across this land. So let my faith define me, not you.

-MykeG

Photograph by James Cooley III

Marsha Mills

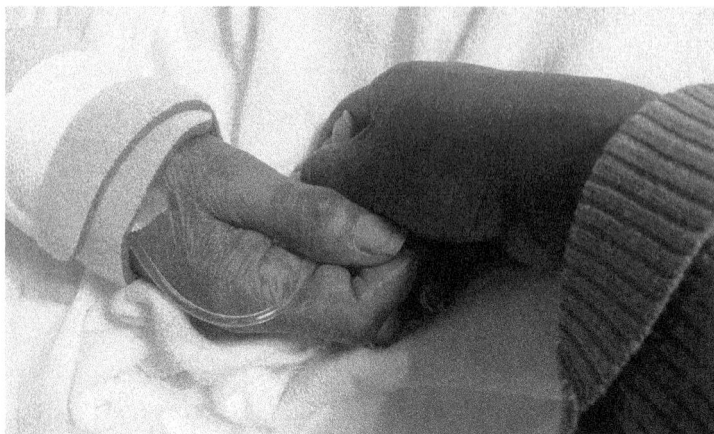

March 30, 2015
In loving memory of my mother,
Odessa M. Greene

Ode to the Hands Of the One I Love

With loving hands
She held me when I could not hold myself.
She bathed me and cared for me when I could
not care for myself.

With swift hand
She delivered discipline
Keeping me within my bounds
Wiping my tears when I met disappointment
When I first faced ridicule
Felt the sting of heart
And the burn of Injustice.

With a generous hand
She bore my financial burden until I was
strong enough to bear my own
And even then she was still there--hand
extended.
With hands of legacy, she cupped the faces of
her grandchildren
Kissed ever so lightly their foreheads as she
handed them the very first Bible
Unappreciated at the time with true value to
be revealed over time.

With hands of reverence
She lifted them to Jesus and prayed
Name by name and heart by heart
From her mouth to God's ear she prayed for
each of us.

With weary hand
She reached for mine--the stronger, the more
stable
For balance for surety
As her steps grew slower and shorter,
She squeezed my hand as a symbol of her
trust in me--her daughter.

With sorrow-filled hand,
I reached out for hers for she could no longer
reach out for mine.
I held her hand when she could no longer
hold mine

I cared for her for as she could no longer care for herself
I prayed with her and for her as she taught me to do.

She could no longer squeeze my hand, but I trusted that she knew I would be there until the end.

-Marsha Mills

Roses or Nails

Roses birth from the Earth
Nourished by the rain and the sun
Slowly, slowly evolving
Growing and blossoming
Creating and becoming
symbol of love renewed.

Nails fall to the Earth discarded
Decayed by rain and sun
Slowly, slowly evolving
Shrinking and rusting
Disintegrating and unwanted
Once used to build, now a tragic memory
and devastating loss.

Which will you be for my heart?
A rose or a nail?
For my heart is as the Earth
a resting place for your intention.

Marsha Mills

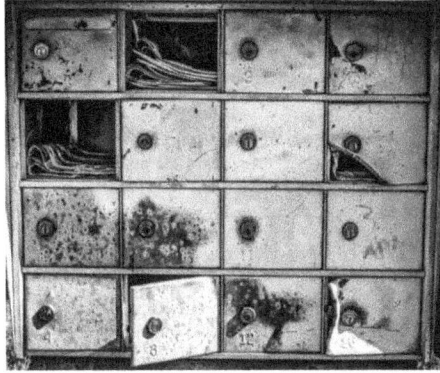

Photograph by James Cooley III

Know Me

You think you know me,
But you don't know me.
For to know me is to lay down self and
crawl into this umber skin
To live this life, and breathe this air and
carry this burden of secrets and regrets
locked deep within.
Opportunities lost, never to come again
Victories won and challenges overcome to the
attentive audience of one.
You see, you don't know me.
Because to know me is to pry open doors,
That hang on rusty hinges
And pick locks that have no key

Cutting fingers on sharp bent edges
Bruised, beaten and bleeding life's oil
You must read lines and lines of fragmented,
broken pieces of unfinished poems
Carry the guilt like a lead albatross of the
thoughts
and whispers of inspiration
You allowed to slip from your grasp
All in hopes of capturing a moment in time
A time in life.
A life in eternity.
That was never meant to be harnessed by the
meager tools of this mind, this paper, and this
pen.
You think you know me
But you have no idea of
The pain behind this smile
The tears behind this laugh
The lies behind this truth
The emptiness behind these doors
You don't know me.
For to know me is to lose you.
And then and only then will you get a small,
fleeting glimpse of knowing me.

Marsha Mills

The Key

Photograph by James Cooley III

It is dark here
The dirt blocks my sight
It covers the windows and chokes out the
light
The air is heavy and thick like sludge
I can't breathe
I can't see
I can't move
I can't budge
I struggle desperately flailing like a drowning
child
Gasping for air to fill my lungs
Only to have it drop like lead to my gut
I want freedom from my captor, and I'm
looking for the key

I need the answer to this puzzle so I can
finally be free
The walls are too high to climb
The windows too distant to reach
The darkness has hampered my eyesight
The sickness has weakened my speech
For years I've been trapped here
In this concrete tomb
Hoping to live to see the day
When I'm reborn from the womb
To accept that I am my own captor
And no key is required for me
All I have to do is get up and open the door
And just like that, I'll be set free
But for now captivity is safer
Complaining comes easier
and Freedom scares me
more than being here
searching hopelessly for the key.

Marsha Mills

Photograph by Erika Blackmon

Sarah Platt

Red Velvet Dreams

Stolen nights
in cheap hotels,
cigarette burns
on the sheets,
red wine
licked from fingertips,
lipstick smeared
across skin;
a poem on the streets,
put to music
behind closed doors.
He's on my to-do list,
my to-use list,
my to-love and to-lose list;
This is where we like to meet,
away from prying eyes,
where skin can meet skin,
rug burn and fingernail scratches
leave braille across our backs,
spelling out all the ways
we're trying to learn how to be free again...
Dawn light peeking through the cracked
curtains,
stretching across our cold, bare skin,

resting on the white rose
he left on my dresser.

-Sarah Platt

Muse II

You were rebellion
and I was truth.
I set you free
to be
everything
I refused,
and I waited
with open arms
for your return –
my prodigal muse.

-Sarah Platt

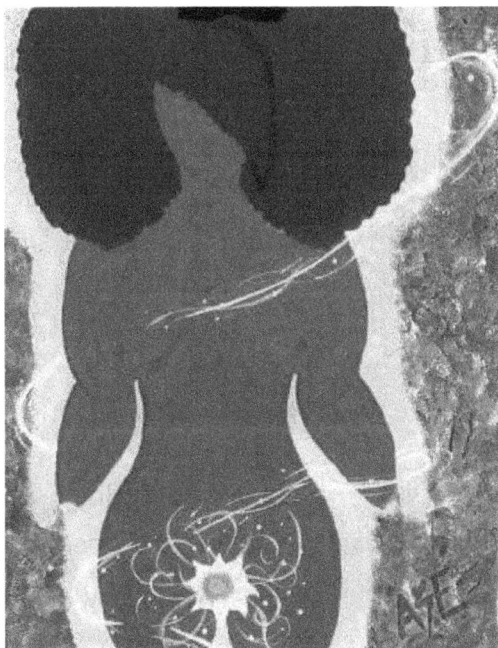

Artist- Tiera Ball. Tiera painted live during a Main St. Monday session. The poets created poems while watching her painting evolve.

Laura Brown

Muse I

The Breakup

Our separation was cordial
A 20-year sentence of silence
I don't remember her voice, her touch,
her taste, her smell
I drifted...
I was ashamed of my muse
She no longer fit my New Life (I thought not,
anyway)
My muse was sexy, sassy, witty, bold,
outrageous, and slick

Ah,

       now

          I

              remember!

Perhaps we can reconcile?

There is no residue of anger or bitterness
Maybe a tinge of sorrow
(mine, hers, or both?)
Must I seek her forgiveness for the rejection
and neglect?
Do I bring my dust cloth,
overflowing
with ink-stained tears
filled with a longing to reconnect?
She's sat on her assigned shelf of neglect and
rejection
gently reminding of things I'm drawn to...
hoping to be drawn out
Her brightly colored garment,
once fashioned with brilliant shades
of a rainbow palette,
is now muted by the harsh light of neglect...

-Laura Brown

Red Velvet Dreams

You know it takes chocolate to make Red
Velvet right?
You are the chocolate foundation to the
sweet stickiness in my bowl
I cannot be stirred by weak and feeble spoons
They would break under the weight of my
stickiness
Red Velvet dreams... of the heated oven
set at 350 degrees,
Properly preheated of course
Red Velvet dreams of the rise
only time and heat can create
Better let Red Velvet cool down before you
cover it with cream...
cheese frosting that is...
Spin it, slice it, plate it right
Time is irrelevant because
Red Velvet Dreams are not only for night
                                        -Laura Brown

Photograph by James Cooley III

Keys

With my hands on my hips and fire in my
mouth
I demanded he return his key...to ME
I am denying him access, revoking his
privileges, changing the locks
His eviction notice is printed in the center of
my eyes and the curl of my lips
With my head held high, I thought to myself
"Yeah, he'll miss the warmth of **MY** space,
the luxury of **THIS** place...
Until... he smiled that easy grin and
opened those expansive hands
FULL
of
keys...

to other warm spaces and luxurious places
and with a voice, laced with silk, he whispered,
"Darlin', 'when you find **YOUR** key, take it
And, being a gracious guest, you see,
he thanked me for my hospitality...
So, when the doctor removes my key from his
eye
and he's no longer on his anesthetic high
Tell him I said, "you're welcome."
and remind him
Keys are a dangerous thing.

-Laura Brown

The Terror That Has No Name

Unseen

  Unheard

    Uncounted

     Uncovered

      Unnamed

       Unclaimed

      Undone

The TERROR that has no name...

   To be unloved

       By anyone

-Laura Brown

Muse II

The Reconciliation

The break up was quick, yet painful
I tried to act like I didn't care...
Until I actually believed my lie
She waited, staying faithful
Whispering my name so her voice would
remain,
etched,
in my soul
While I cheated with plastic inspiration
Exchanged the untamed and exotic unknown
for docile ink pets of perfect meter and rhyme
Yet, upon hearing my pen call her name
she soared, hurdled,
bravely from her dusty shelf

To save me from the blank page
which threatened my sanity
She never asked for an apology
or an explanation
She was simply content to be invited
to dance with my pen once again
Like makeup sex on ink-stained sheets...
of
Paper

-Laura Brown

Lusonda
T. Jennings

My Favorite Muse

When I hear you, my spirit is calmed
When I see you, my body begins to jump
When I experience you, I want to go deeper
My thoughts differ, my soul quivers, and I just want you nearer
I often ask myself what would life be without your presence
Empty, confusing, chaotic, lack of serene essence
I need you especially when I'm going through
My mind craves you, and I love the way you encourage me to move
Music, o music you are my peace
The very sound of you helps clarify the words I speak
The words I write love, to begin with your beat
Living without you would cause more pain in my journey
I love how you do me, and I know you feel it when we are together
Music I needed you then, I need you now, I need you always and forever

-Luronda T. Jennings

48

What If My Photograph Could Talk Back to Me?

Hey there beautiful juicy girl, I'm so excited to be in your world
You looked at your smile and fell in love with the child you were created to be
Who me?
Yes, you, looking all good as the new you
I see past those lost pounds because I knew you back when you struggled to walk a mile
You see your appearance is nice, but that mindset change is just right
Yep right where it needs to be to keep elevating me
Let me suggest to you to keep falling in love with your smile
Because I know your smile helps you push through that mile of that journey that reflects that child you were created to be...living a life of faith purposefully.

-Luronda T. Jennings

Red Velvet Dreams

Smooth, sensual, savory, and sweet
Yes, sometimes salty but your demeanor
always encourages me to speak
Sweep me off my feet with your mind, yes I
love the way you think
I often think about you before I close los ojos
Then I wake with mi rojo pen in hand writing
about the smoothness of your devotion
Smooth like velvet, rojo mi amore
It's you who I adore, my reality not forced to
dream anymore
Because you knocked at the door of my heart,
not my pants
You took my hands and caressed my mind in
advance
Without a notice, you moved back in
Sending chills down my spine and a brighter
tone to my skin
A deeper meaning to my grin, a slower tempo
to my spin, because I don't want to rush this
rojo amore or come to an end
Once my red velvet dream, now your actual
presence defines the true meaning of happily
ever after in a horse and carriage

Mi rojo amore is way beyond average
His being provides a deeper meaning to the
release of white doves...peace, joy, love, and
happiness
Mi rojo amore, let's have a toast to not
dreaming anymore
Dreams are cool, but I'd rather drool over my
reality of the tragedy of dreaming no more
With my knees to the floor and my head to
the sky, thank You Lord for creating mi rojo
amore
My inspiration of my red velvet dreams, now
my reality...dreaming. no. more.

-Luronda T. Jennings

False Perception

(Inspired by the picture of the keys taken by James

Cooley III)

I've never really understood the saying, "What you see is what you get."

When clearly one's perception may be inaccurate

One's perception could be blinded by the wear and tear of the cover of the book

Vision blurred, judgment cast, without flipping a page or taking a second look

A deeper look on the inside not just a close minded peek

You can't possibly know me just by my outer capacity

My inner will explain the cause of every tear from every tragedy

And once you open that door you'll understand the light that shines from every victory

So for me what you see is NOT what you get

It's not until you open the door, to see the real me

Then don't be scared to snatch the door from the hinges, crawl in, take a seat, open my book, flip each page with an open mind, and you'll find that what you saw on the outside, doesn't begin to compare to the inside...a true gem, a work of art, the definition of one of a kind

-Luronda T. Jennings

Mindset Empowers Everything

I finally realized that my mindset is more
productive outside of that box
Little did I know how much of my potential
was being blocked
Now I have power over my thoughts with my
purpose more defined
Everything is more stable from the power I've
given my mind
Please understand how much power the mind
contains
I encourage you to open up to allowing your
mind to refrain
Refrain from the empty thoughts of endless
depression
In order to sustain the thoughts of positive
obsession
Obsession with becoming a better you, doing
exactly what you know you need to do, when
you need to do, how you need to do, where
you need to do, giving your very best...I mean
all of you!

Refrain from becoming concerned with the
hatred of others, for the power is placed in
you for YOU to uncover
Uncover it now don't wait any longer, there is
so much in store with little time to slumber
The power of your mindset empowers
everything
So get up and get in the game before the bell
rings
Because if you don't, there's a possibility you
may miss out on this thing
There are only so many opportunities He will
present I mean
Now do you the realize the power of your
thinking?
Refrain from pity, wipe your tears, face your
fears, and unleash the powerful thinking
The thinking from your mindset that will take
your life to another place
The place you never imagined but your
mindset has prepared you to face
Face it all full force knowing your mindset has
your back
There's so much positive strength in your
words and there's no need for physical attacks

Empowered by your thoughts and
replenished by The love
You should forever be reaching toward all
that's above
For your mindset truly empowers everything
In order for you to face whatever it is this life
may bring

-Luronda T. Jennings

Invitation to Create

Describe the hands of the person you love.

_____

_____

_____

_____

_____

_____

_____

_____

_____

_____

_____

_____

_____

_____

_____

_____

_____

_____

_____

_____

_____

_____

Describe the smells you remember as a child

_____

_____

_____

_____

_____

_____

_____

_____

_____

_____

_____

_____

_____

_____

_____

_____

_____

_____

_____

_____

_____

_____

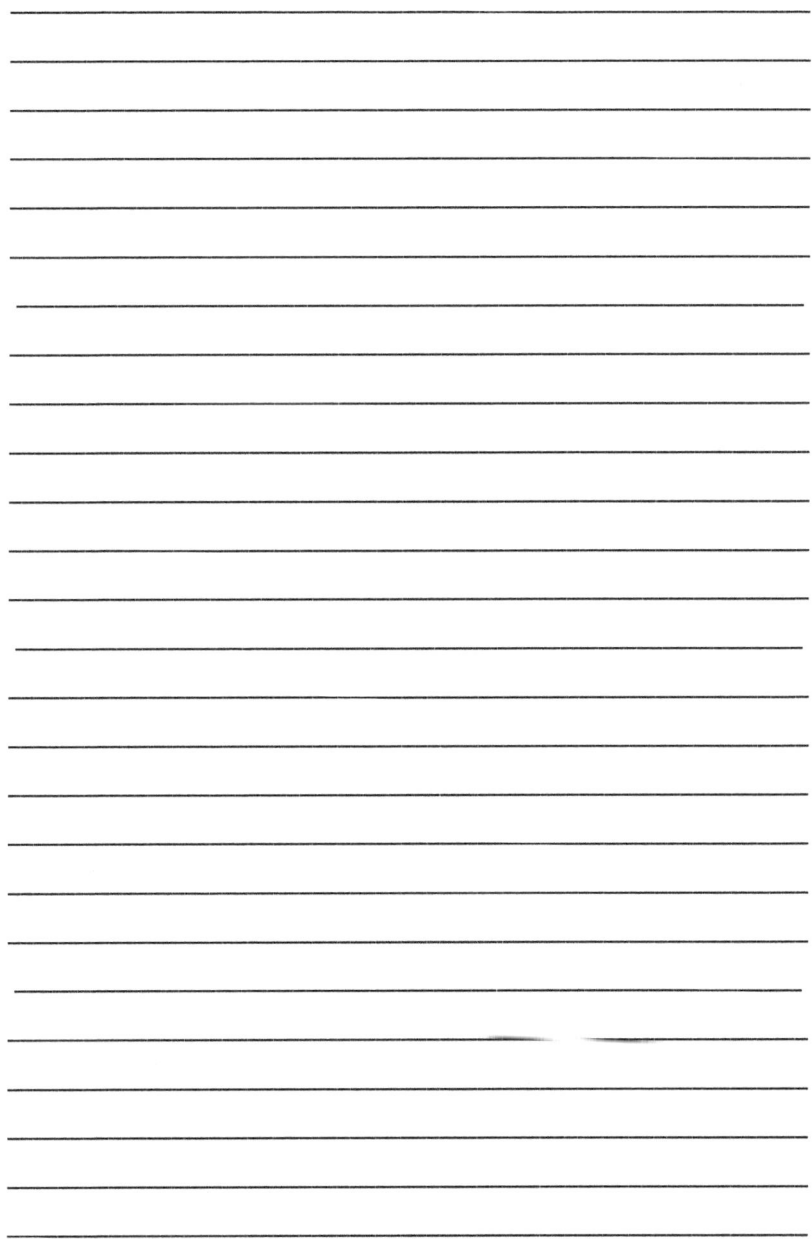

What does love sound like?

_____

_____

_____

_____

_____

_____

_____

_____

_____

_____

_____

_____

_____

_____

_____

_____

_____

_____

_____

_____

Describe your muse.

_____

_____

_____

_____

_____

_____

_____

_____

_____

_____

_____

_____

_____

_____

_____

_____

_____

_____

_____

_____

_____

_____

About the Poets

Erika Blackmon

Books filled her home so she could never be alone. Encyclopedias and dictionaries are a gathering of her friends...words.

She met poetry in a fifth-grade class. The discipline of the art made her want to pass it...on and just write...but her teacher saw talent despite her closed off nature. The teacher kept exposing the stanzas. As the young became older, she found her poetic voice. ...But life happened, motherhood took center stage. Erika continued to write with a different muse, a new inspiration, letting the words soar like a kite. As she returned to the stage, she performed everywhere even in places she dares not say, eventually creating a safe place by hosting shows on that legendary black stage. Erika, a mother, a poet and creator has become a humble part of the performing community in Chattanooga by creating shows to highlight local creatives. She is also one of the creators of the popular show **Poetic KamaSutra**. Erika is one of the rotating hosts for **The FLOOR is YOURS.**

She is a successful workshop creator and facilitator of her production company, Velvet Poetry Productions. Erika created Main St. Mondays workshop to allow writers a safe place to revive the poet within and renew their passion for writing. Contact Erika at

dionneblackmon189@gmail.com

Mychael Greene

Mychael (MykeG) Greene was born in Chattanooga, TN. He was influenced to change the world as an artist, by listening to the lyrics and inspirational words from Michael Jackson. As a child, he sat in front of the television mimicking his moves and watching the crowd get excited about his performances which lead to him creating the lifelong *slogan "Every Lion Has Its Roar"* which means no matter where or who you are, your voice can change the world for the better.

 "It was all a dream," said perfectly by Notorious B.I.G. was the highlight quote that kept Mychael moving towards his dreams and goals. Picturing his mothers, fathers, family, and those who inspired him to write poetry is his way of showing gratitude to them and the

world, and he's not ashamed to let people know how much he loves them.

Mychael attended Middle Tennessee State University and majored in Exercise Science but had a deeper love for poetry. He has performed in front of crowds in Murfreesboro with a creative group called **Word Up** and in Chattanooga with **Rhyme N Chatt**. This artist is a man who almost lost it all but turned it into loving all, and he gives all praise to God for it. So he asks, always with a smile on his face, *"Without God Where Would I Be?"*.

You can contact Mychael at:
Snapchat: mykeg_thepoet
Instagram: @mykeg_thepoet
Facebook: Mychael Jamoson Greene
Email: mykegpoetry@gmail.com

Marsha Mills

Marsha Mills is a Chattanooga native and current president of the local poetry group, **Rhyme N Chatt Interactive Poetry Organization**, which has provided an outlet for local poets to share their work since 1999.

Her poetry is reality laced with a touch of sass. She is poetically known as The Poetic Diva because she often mixes vocal melodies and rhythms to her poetic renderings.

She enjoys using poetry to encourage and inspire others. Marsha's passion is the birthing of new poets and writers, especially our youth. She encourages others to step out of their comfort zone and give voice to their poetry. Marsha is also a member of **The Voices of THECREATIVEUNDERGROUND** and the gospel singing group, **Divinely Favored**.

Email: jermor6@gmail.com

Facebook: MarshaThePoeticDiva

Sarah Platt

Sarah Platt is a local poet and children's book author. You can check out more of her work at
www.lulu.com/spotlight/imapoetandiknowit1

Laura Brown

Laura Brown is an Author, Speaker, Teacher, Publishing Coach, and Creative Strategist. She is the director of the **Serious Writers' Accountability Training (S.W.A.T.) Camp**, where she helps aspiring authors, create their literary legacies. Laura is the author of **"Delighting in the Law of the Lord- Psalm 119 DevArtJournal" and "Color Me Delighted-Psalm 119 Coloring Book",** which are available on Amazon and at Barnes and Nobles.

She is a native of Toledo, Ohio and now resides in Chattanooga, TN. She is married to retired Air Force Chief, Wayne Brown and they have three children and two grand-children. She enjoys all things creative and loves to plan "Pop Pop & Nanna Surprise Adventures" for her granddaughters.

Stay tuned for her forthcoming book of poetry **"Full Circle- The Evolution of a Muse"**.

For more information about The S.W.A.T. Book Camp go to www.swatbookcamp.com or Contact Laura at coachlaurabrown@gmail.com 423-402-9317

Luronda T. Jennings

Luronda T. Jennings, M.Ed., is the Founder, Executive Director, and Licensed Special Educator at Journey Educational Services, Inc. (J.E.S.). J.E.S. is a 501c3 non-profit organization that provides academic and behavioral supplemental services to school-aged students with disabilities. Luronda founded this organization in April 2015 after 10 years of teaching in various schools. She is passionate about educating the minds of our future. She also works as the part-time College Advisor at CSAS, her alma mater. In her spare time, Luronda loves to write poetry, listen to music, paint, and enjoy quality time with her loved ones.

She has been writing poetic expressions since the age of 15 and looks forward to becoming an author of poetic children's books, special education curriculum, and motivational books.

In the last three years, Luronda has learned the true meaning of living by faith and not by sight. She finally gave herself permission to permanently bury fear and is now allowing God and faith to lead her to her destiny.

Contact Luronda at

Email – rising2succeed@gmail.com

Phone – 423-774-3444

9 781941 749647